A Biblical Guide to

DEFEATING DEPRESSION

SUZANNE PHILLIPPA MARCELLUS
Founder and President of
HOUSE OF PROTECTION, INC.

Editor:	Phillip Washington Fender
Cover Design:	Teodore Thomas
Illustrator:	Alecia Rodriguez, Insatgram @ aleciarodriguez_inc
Photo on Back:	Jeaneane Swaby, ThruJensEyes
ISBN-13:	978-1-7331592-2-7

Introduction

House of Protection, Inc. is pleased to provide, **A Biblical Guide to Defeating Depression**, as one of our Overcoming Life's Obstacles Courses, which provide Biblical guidance to overcome life's difficult issues.

Over the next six weeks, you will Identify, Unmask, find Relief from and be Equipped to fight depression's emotional, physical and spiritual effects. As you exchange your pain for the pleasures found in Christ, you will become empowered to renew your mind.

This guide is ideal for small groups, ages 12 and up, as there are several group based discussions offered; but will also be of great benefit to you, individually.

Table of Contents

Lesson 1:
"Identifying Depression"

Objectives:
1. Define Depression.
2. Identify Depression in your life.
3. Discuss the first two steps in Defeating Depression.

Let us unravel Depression, as we identify its effects on us emotionally, physically and spiritually. Our ultimate goal is to gain the tools needed to Defeat Depression. Every war consists of mini battles, in the past you may have lost a mini battle to depression, but you did not lose the war. The God we serve gives us victory through our faith in Jesus Christ!

"For whatever is born of God overcomes the world: And this is the victory that overcometh the world, even our faith." 1 John 5:4

"These things I have spoken unto you, that in Me ye may have peace. In the world ye shall have tribulation: but be of good cheer, I have overcome the world." John 16:33

The Merriam Webster Online Dictionary (MWOD), defines Depression as an *act of depressing* or a *state of being depressed*: such as feeling sad, dejected, or having a mood disorder marked especially by sadness, inactivity, difficulty in thinking and concentration, a significant increase or decrease in appetite, time spent sleeping, feelings of dejection and hopelessness an sometimes suicidal tendencies.

Have you experienced any of these **Emotional Signs** of depression? (Definitions are taken from MWOD)

- ☐ Brokenhearted (overcome by grief or despair)
- ☐ Despondent (feeling or showing extreme discouragement, dejection or depression)
- ☐ Downcast/Dejected/Gloomy (low in spirits)
- ☐ Grieving (experience deep and poignant distress caused by or as if by bereavement)
- ☐ Hopeless (having no expectation of good or success: Despairing)
- ☐ Melancholy (suggestive or expressive of sadness or depression of mind or spirit)
- ☐ Miserable (being in a pitiable state of distress or unhappiness, as from want or shame)
- ☐ Mournful (expressing sorrow, full of sorrow)
- ☐ Oppressed (to burden spiritually or mentally: weigh heavily upon)
- ☐ Sadness (affected with or expressive of grief or unhappiness)
- ☐ Sorrowful (full of deep distress, sadness, or regret especially for the loss of someone or something loved
- ☐ Suicidal (dangerous especially to life, destructive to one's own interests)
- ☐ Wretched (Deeply afflicted, dejected, or distressed in body or mind)

Have you experienced any of these **Physical Signs** of depression?

- ☐ Difficulty in thinking and concentrating.
- ☐ Inactivity (absence of activity or effort).
- ☐ Increase or Decrease in Appetite.
- ☐ Increase or Decrease in Time spent sleeping.

Have you experienced any of these **Spiritual Signs** of depression?

- ☐ Belief that God does not hear you when you pray.
- ☐ Belief that there is no purpose in your existence.
- ☐ Belief that your failure has disqualified you for your purpose.
- ☐ Feeling that God has left you.
- ☐ Feeling that God does not love or care about you.
- ☐ Feeling that you will never be forgiven.
- ☐ Hopelessness in your eternal destination.
- ☐ Inability to pray.
- ☐ Inability to praise and worship (Sing, dance, clap your hands, and shout to the Lord.)
- ☐ Tired in your faith and service to God.

Over the course of our lives we all experience some type of grief or sadness, however to identify depression, there are two main questions we must answer.

1. Is it temporary? Are these negative physical, emotional and spiritual experiences lasting for an hour, a day, maybe a few days? Or...

2. Is it continual? Are these negative physical, emotional and spiritual experiences lasting for more than two weeks at a time, lasting for months at a times, even years?

The length of time our battles last with sadness determine how many people we need to invite on the battlefield with us. The longer the battle, the more warriors you need on the field. God never intended us to fight any battle alone.

➤ **Emotionally**, Holy Spirit serves as our comforter and Jesus as our intercessor, who empathizes with our weaknesses.
➤ **Physically**, He has given us each other to: pray, be an understanding ear, an encouraging voice, an accountability partner, a wise counselor, a faith filled doctor, a well-studied nutritionist and the list can go on.
➤ **Spiritually**, He has given us Salvation through Jesus, His Holy Spirit, and His Word. As well as the assistance of angels.

The Latin word depressus, where we get the word depressed from, means to PRESS DOWN. It is difficult to fight this battle on your own, because it literally feels like a physical, emotional and spiritual weight pressing you down, causing you to think that you are unable to lift your hands and move forward.

Exodus 17 records a battle between Amalek and Israel. As men were on the battlefield, Moses, Aaron and Hur stood on the top of a hill. Moses held the rod of God in his hand as they fought, if his hands were raised, Israel prevailed, when he let own his hands Amalek prevailed. Let's pick up at verses 12-13:
But Moses' hands were heavy; and they took a stone and put it under him, and he sat thereon; and Aaron and Hur stayed up his hands, the one on the one side, and the other on the other side; and his hands were steady until the going down of the sun. 13 And Joshua discomfited Amalek and his people with the edge of the sword.

The first two steps needed to defeat Depression are:
1. **Remove Your Mask.**
2. **Seek out a Support System.**

REMOVE YOUR MASK.

Do you wear a "mask" to hide your true feelings and emotions? For example, when you are very sad, instead of being transparent with your friends, do you wear a smile? If yes, at that moment your smile becomes your mask. We have learned to wear many masks, for different reasons, some may be:

☐ For the comfort of those around us.

☐ We don't want to become the center of attention or alter the mood of the crowd.

☐ We're not sure if anyone cares enough to listen, and even if they did listen, we're not convinced that would change anything.

☐ Sometimes, we just don't want to confront our reality, we would rather pretend, making it easier to deny our present circumstance.

Let's think about the type of masks you have worn? (Confident mask, Religious mask, Polite mask, Positivity mask, Humility mask, Love mask, Anger mask to hide your sadness...)

_____

_____

Draw a face of the overall emotion you experienced today. It can be a simple, happy, sad, confused, scared face, etc...

Now draw what others saw as your emotion.

[Empty box for drawing]

Were you transparent in sharing your joy or pain, or were you pretending?

_____

_____

Before we can be real with anyone else, we must be real with ourselves. There are times when I have been hurt or offended and found myself saying, "I'm ok", when I really was not ok. In my quest to be polite, not embarrass myself or seem weak, I have often chosen to wear masks.

It is important to identify when you are wearing a mask and it is beneficial to be attentive to when those around you could be possibly doing the same.

Group Activity (15 minutes)
Discuss a few famous men and women who committed suicide, whom you were shocked to learn about. Since they always seemed to be smiling, telling jokes, and appeared to have everything they could need. Do you think their story would have ended differently, had they taken off their mask?

_____

_____

10

Choose to remove your mask(s). Don't be afraid, God already sees, hears and knows your pain. You don't have to try to hide it from Him.

SEEK OUT A SUPPORT SYSTEM

Ask God for courage and discernment. We need courage to stop hiding and discernment on who to trust. Who can you trust, to share how you have been feeling? Is it a friend, spouse, relative, Pastor?

List a few people you will consider being transparent with and commit to contact them. Tell them exactly what you need. Moses knew he needed help keeping his hands raised and was humble enough to receive the help.

_____

_____

_____

Note: *If you have no one's name written, please speak with your group facilitator at the end of this lesson. If you are going through this guide individually and need someone to speak with, consider scheduling a complimentary Biblical teletherapy appointment at www.houseofprotection.org.*

Now, list some ways that someone can assist you on this battlefield. For example, sometimes I need someone to just listen and not say things like, "It's going to be ok", "Don't cry about that", and "Just get over it". What do you need? Look back at the items you checked off on page 6 and 7 regarding Physical, Emotional and Spiritual signs of depression, to help you get ideas.

Assistance on the Battlefield List

_____

_____

_____

_____

_____

_____

_____

_____

Group Activity (15 minutes)
Discuss your Assistance on the Battlefield List to get additional ideas from one another.

In summary, be mindful of any emotional, physical and spiritual changes you may experience. Choose to be real with yourself and with your support system. Help others help you, by identifying your needs.

Let's pray.

Heavenly Father, You see the times where I have experienced heaviness of heart and felt unable to find joy. Cause my hope and joy to be found in You. Lift the weight of sadness and depression, surround me with trustworthy friendships. Teach me how to have a fruitful relationship with your Holy Spirit and to utilize the spiritual and natural tools you have given me, in Jesus name.

Lesson 2:
"Unmasking Depression, disguised as Goliath"

<u>Review</u>
In the previous lesson, we defined depression, identified its operation in our lives emotionally, physically and spiritually; and chose to, remove our mask(s) & seek out a support system.

☐ Have you worked on removing your mask(s)?
☐ Did you contact the people, whose names you wrote down and ask them to join your team?

Remember:

The length of time our battles last with sadness determine how many people we need to invite on the battlefield with us. The longer the battle, the more warriors you need on the field. God never intended us to fight any battle alone. (Lesson 1 p.7)

Objectives:
1. Confront Depression.
2. Adjust Your Perspective.
3. Jesus Can Heal Your Heart and Brain.

CONFRONT DEPRESSION

In 1 Samuel 17 we read an account of great fear and dismay that came upon the armies of Israel, when they were challenged by the heavily armored giant Philistine named, Goliath.

"8 ... Choose a man for yourselves, and let him come down to me. 9 If he is able to fight with me and kill me, then we will be your servants. But if I prevail against him and kill him, then you shall be our servants and serve us." 10 And the Philistine said, "I defy the armies of Israel this day; give me a man, that we may

fight together." 11 When Saul and all Israel heard these words of the Philistine, they were dismayed and greatly afraid."

Depression is a bully, like Goliath, inflicting deep feelings of discouragement and fear. It has the ability to make you feel destitute, feeble, insignificant and hopeless, as it rises in size and stature before you.

Depression requires you to think it is bigger than Christ in you. It wants to prophesy that it will always rule over you.

We must believe the promise of 1 John 4:4, *"You are of God, little children, and have overcome them, because **He who is in you is greater than he who is in the world**."*

Speak the following out loud:
Depression must bow to Christ!
Depression will not rule over my life!
Jesus, you are the ruler of my life!

For forty days both morning and evening, Goliath taunted God's people. They would armor up and head out to fight the Philistines, but as soon as Goliath showed up, they trembled and ran in fear. (Verses 20-24)

Their armor represents the mask(s) we wear. They appeared bold, confident and ready for battle, but in reality, they were full of fear and horror.

We must first be honest with ourselves before we can be honest with anyone else.

14

Jesus does not want us dependent on the mask(s). We can rely on Him to bring the continual healing, courage and joy we need to remove our masks.

> *Jesus has the power to destroy your masks.*
> *He gives you the courage to face your giants.*
> *And in Christ, you have the Victory!*

At times, we seem to have the ability and courage to overcome life's obstacles, without blinking an eye. Yet, when confronted with situations seemingly outside of our control and beyond our ability to handle, we are tempted to cower.

ADJUST YOUR PERSPECTIVE

The only one who did not cower in the face of Goliath was David, the shepherd boy; who was sent by his father to check on his three eldest brothers and deliver food to them. David showed up in time to hear Goliath's challenge, witness the armies of Israel run away and learn of the reward King Saul was offering to anyone who could defeat him. *"Then David spoke to the men who stood by him, saying... "For who is this uncircumcised Philistine, that he should defy the armies of the living God?" (1 Samuel 17:26)*

David, (whom Christ came from his lineage), would later become King, **stepped on the scene with a different perspective** than King Saul and the entire army. David recognized that although Goliath was larger than he and the others, Goliath was no match for God.

Speak the following out loud:
Depression is smaller than GOD!
GOD is bigger than depression!

There is Power in Perspective.
Adjusting your perspective affects your
circumstance.

As your perspective is adjusted, don't be distracted by those whose vision remain the same. Not everyone will understand your faith in God, to put the tools in your hand needed to gain the victory over your giants. David's eldest brother Eliab, was angry at David. He accused him of being prideful, insolent and nosey. Deep down I'm sure Eliab was jealous of his youngest brother's courage but when weighing what was at stake (the freedom of Israel), there must have been a part of him that wanted to rejoice in his brother's boldness at that time, but did not know how to.

CAUTION:

Be careful of those, who do not motivate you to be victorious. They may get angry at you or become doubtful because they have not found the boldness and courage to defeat the giants in their own lives.

Then David said to Saul, "Let no man's heart fail because of him; your servant will go and fight with this Philistine." And Saul said to David, "You are not able to go against this Philistine to fight with him; for you are a youth, and he a man of war from his youth." (1 Samuel 17:32-33)

David saw the discouragement of the people. They were not just men tired and hungry from being on the battlefield without relief for forty days, but men whose hearts had failed. Solomon (David's son) wrote in Proverbs 18:14, *"The spirit of a man will sustain him in sickness, but **who can bear a broken spirit**?"* When we suffer from a broken spirit or a broken heart, it is the most challenging to overcome, while driving some to commit suicide.

Depression is a fruit of brokenness. It drains you of your physical and mental strength and takes away your drive to fight. By being aware of depression's strategies, we can guard our hearts.

"Keep thy heart with all diligence; for out of it are the issues of life." Proverbs 4:23

Those who struggle with depression should be handled with care. He or she may become afraid and anxious of the next minute, hour and day, because they do not feel strong enough to face its' victories and disappointments.

"For God hath not given us the spirit of fear; but of power, and of love, and of a sound mind."
2 Timothy 1:7

The battle of depression is won with the intercession (intervention) of others, make sure you ask your Support System to pray.

Romans 8:34 shares a wonderful truth, Jesus is our intercessor. *"Who is he who condemns? It is **Christ** who died, and furthermore is also risen, who is even at the right hand of God, who also **makes intercession for us**."*

David, a child, stood in the gap as an intercessor for the Kingdom of Israel, although his ability, faith and strength were initially doubted. He recalled to Saul, the victories God had given him, while protecting his father's sheep.

"Your servant has killed both lion and bear; and this uncircumcised Philistine will be like one of them..." Moreover David said, "The LORD, *who delivered me from the paw of the lion and from the paw of the bear, He will deliver me from the hand of this Philistine." And Saul said to David, "Go, and the* LORD *be with you!" 1 Samuel 17:26-37*

Surround yourself with people who have great faith in the power of God!
Those who have experienced victories over their giants and believe God will do it again!

Speak the following out loud:

God will deliver me from Depression!
God will deliver my family from depression!
God will deliver my friends from depression!

So how did this battle with the Philistines end? Victoriously! *"Then David said to the Philistine, "You come to me with a sword, with a spear, and with a javelin.* **But I come to you in the name of the** LORD **of hosts, the God of the armies of Israel**, *whom you have defied.* ⁵⁰ *So David prevailed over the Philistine with a sling and a stone, and struck the Philistine and killed him... 1 Samuel 17:45, 50*

David used the name of the Lord and the tools God provided for him (a sling and a stone) to defeat Goliath! Proverbs 18:10 declares, *"The name of the Lord is a strong tower: the righteous runneth into it, and is safe."*

Group Activity (15 minutes)

Discuss the following two questions and write your personal answer.

Do you believe in the power of the name of Jesus?

_____

_____

_____

Do you believe that your emotional and physical battles belong to the Lord?

_____

_____

_____

JESUS CAN HEAL YOUR HEART AND BRAIN

The battle of Depression takes place in the heart and mind. In treating depression, doctors will suggest therapy and sometimes prescribe an antidepressant, which increases the production of serotonin, a chemical naturally produced in our brain.

When fighting the HEART battle, we must:

☐ **Believe Jesus is the healer of the broken hearted.**

The LORD is near to those who have a broken heart, and saves such as have a contrite spirit.
Psalm 34:18 (NKJV)

He healeth the broken in heart, and bindeth up their wounds. Psalm 147:3

But he was wounded for our transgressions, he was bruised for our iniquities: the chastisement of our peace was upon him; and with his stripes we are healed. Isaiah 53:5

☐ **Learn to encourage ourselves, by reminding ourselves of who God is.**

"God is our refuge and strength, a very present help in trouble." Psalm 46:1

☐ **Put our Hope in God.**

Why art thou cast down, O my soul? and why art thou disquieted within me? hope thou in God: for I shall yet praise him, who is the health of my countenance, and my God.
Psalm 42:11 & 43:5

When fighting the BRAIN battle, it may feel more complicated. You want to receive the encouragement of good counsel, but your body won't allow you to be happy and hopeful. Doctors recognize that the shortage of serotonin can harvest depression. I challenge you to believe that Jesus is still healing the sick, raising the dead and casting out demons. He is equally in the business of healing our emotional wounds and any physical ailment (this includes our outer body, every organ, cell and chemical inside our body).

"When the even was come, they brought unto him many that were possessed with devils: and he cast out the spirits with his word, and healed all that were sick: That it might be fulfilled which was spoken by Esaias the prophet, saying, Himself took our infirmities, and bare our sicknesses."
Matthew 8:16-17

Walking in healing of both our heart and brain requires *faith, healthy lifestyle practices,* (such as exercising and eating tryptophan filled foods, which help naturally increase serotonin levels), and *having a strong support system.*

Heavenly Father, I come to you in the wonderful name of Jesus believing there is power in His name. I repent for my dependency on the masks I have used for my protection and to hide the truth of my condition. Today, I choose to be real with myself. Please destroy my mask and give me the courage to face my giants. Forgive me of unbelief and increase my faith to expect you to deliver and heal me of all of my emotional, physical and spiritual ailments. Every time my emotions cause my courage to fail, I will remember who You are and trust your plan for my life. Thank you for healing and victory, in Jesus name.

Lesson 3:
"Guided Relief from Depression"

Review

In the previous lesson, as we unmasked depression disguised as Goliath, we learned:

- ☐ To change our perspective. *Depression is smaller than GOD! GOD is BIGGER than depression!*
- ☐ To depend on Jesus and not our masks.
- ☐ The intercession of others, help us win the battle with depression, so we must ask others to pray.
- ☐ God can heal you of depression that stems from the heart or from the brain.

Objectives:
1. Depend on the Affirmation of God.
2. Remember and Reflect on all God has done.

Today we will work to find relief from depression, through the sons of Korah's writing in Psalm 42.

As the deer pants for the water brooks, so pants my soul for You, O God. ² My soul thirsts for God, for the living God. When shall I come and appear before God? Psalm 42:1-2

When warring with depression, we can become very dependent and needy on the affirmation of others or believe there is no consolation for our sorrow, like a thirst that can never be quenched. It is important to desire the affirmation and comfort from God more than man. Imagine a deer running quickly through the forest from its predator. As it escapes its' enemy, it takes a moment to rest. His panting though cooling his body, is not working fast enough, so he now becomes desperate for water.

We must become desperate (thirsty) for God.

The writers of this Psalm are transparent about their need to hear a response from God about their present need. In John 4:1-42 we witness Jesus weary from His journey. As He takes a seat by a well, He requests a drink of water from a Samaritan woman. During their conversation, Jesus explained:

1. If she knew who He was, she would have asked Him for a drink and He would have given her **living water**. (vs. 10)
2. After drinking His water, a person will **never thirst again** because His water results in **everlasting life**. (vs.14)

As we continue reading this account, we come to learn that this Samaritan woman previously had 5 husbands and was currently living with a man, who she was not married to. Before meeting Jesus, she attempted to fill the longings of her soul with men, but Jesus offered to fill the void in her life that nothing and no one was able to fill.

Heavenly Father, cause our souls to be thirsty for You. Jesus promised us in Mathew 5:6 that if we hunger and thirst for righteousness we shall be filled. Fill us in Jesus name.

My tears have been my food day and night, while they continually say to me, "Where is your God?" Psalm 42:3

The psalmists then express that their source of pain are people's opinions of their relationship with God and God's ability to rescue them. In our moments of pain, there may be times we feel abandoned by God because it feels like He is taking too long to respond to us. It doesn't help when those around us begin to mock us. As we learned in Lesson 1, Depression

(Sadness) can affect our appetite and sleep patterns. These men were experiencing sleepless nights, filled with tears as well as loss of appetite because of their sadness.

Do you have a situation in your life that you are waiting on God to respond to?

_____

_____

Have you had sleepless nights, days when you couldn't eat and tears that you couldn't control?

_____

_____

Have others ridiculed you for your belief as you wait on God to rescue you?

_____

_____

> **When I remember these things, I pour out my soul within me. For I used to go with the multitude; I went with them to the house of God, with the voice of joy and praise, with a multitude that kept a pilgrim feast. Psalm 42:4**

Do you hear the writers' pain? Those who are mocking them, are the same ones that they worshiped and celebrated God with. In their cry to God they remained transparent. They recognized that as often as they remembered the good times, the memories brought them pain.

Are there past relationships that you had, whose good memories now bring pain? Why?

_____

_____

After this confession to God, the psalmists' tone begins to change. They remove their focus and thoughts from the cause of their pain and begin to encourage themselves.

> *Why are you cast down, O my soul? And why are you disquieted within me? Hope in God, for I shall yet praise Him for the help of His countenance. ⁶ O my God, my soul is cast down within me; therefore I will remember You from the land of the Jordan, and from the heights of Hermon, From the Hill Mizar. Psalm 42:5-6*

When feeling down, don't be afraid to ask yourself, "WHY?" and answer honestly. In this verse we note that whatever the WHY may be, *we must never lose HOPE in God.* Amid our distress *we must encourage ourselves to praise God.* The writers' circumstances have not changed, yet they praise Him for the help of His countenance (face or presence). **They set their attention on God's presence and recall all He has done in their lives.**

In times of despair:
1. Identify the source of your pain.
2. Pray, invite God's presence, into your situation.
3. Remind yourself of all God has done for you. This will increase your faith.
4. Focus/meditate on God's face and not your pain.
5. Open your mouth and thank God for everything.

Group Activity (15 minutes)

Identify a specific area of pain in your life. Write a simple prayer, then record one thing Christ has done for you. Choose an attribute about God to focus on that is the solution to your area of concern. Finally, identify one thing, you consider large or small to tell God thank you for. Discuss with group.

For example:

I am hurting because: My family abandoned me.

Prayer: Heavenly Father. I need you step into this place of pain.

I Remember: How I felt your peace surround me, when I was afraid.

Focus: I choose to focus on the fact that you promised never to leave or forsake me.

Praise: Lord, thank you for loving me and caring for my soul.

I am hurting because:

_____

_____

_____

Prayer:

_____

_____

_____

I Remember:

_____

_____

_____

Focus:

_____

_____

_____

Praise:

_____

_____

_____

> **Deep calls unto deep at the noise of Your waterfalls; all Your waves and billows have gone over me. The LORD will command His lovingkindness in the daytime,... Psalm 42:7-8**

The psalmists now move from commanding their souls to:

1. Hope in God
2. Praise God and
3. Remember God

To:

4. Experiencing God

They sense Holy Spirit drawing them to a deeper trust and love for God. Now God's presence is washing over their bodies, hearts and minds. They encourage themselves in the promise that God commands His loving kindness in the morning. In the midst of their tears they acknowledge His loving kindness. When David was in the wilderness of Judah, he wrote Psalm 63:1-3,

> *"O God, You are my God; early will I seek You;*
> *My soul thirsts for You; My flesh longs for You in a*
> *dry and thirsty land where there is no water. ² So I*
> *have looked for You in the sanctuary, to see Your*
> *power and Your glory. ³ Because*
> **Your lovingkindness is better than life,**
> *my lips shall praise You."*

Our Heavenly Father's loving kindness is better than life. David, though thirsty in the wilderness, sets his focus towards God and praises Him for His Lovingkindness.

Speak the following out loud:

Lord thank you for your loving kindness!

> *...and in the night His song shall be with me— A prayer to the God of my life. Psalm 42:8*

At night, they now have the comfort of God's song, which they describe as a prayer. When Paul and Silas were beaten and wrongly imprisoned, at midnight they were praying and singing hymns to the Lord (Acts 16:25-34). Zephaniah 3:17 says that the Lord rejoices over us with singing.

Speak the following out loud:

Lord, let your song be with us, in Jesus name.

> *I will say to God my Rock, "Why have You forgotten me? Why do I go mourning because of the oppression of the enemy?"* 10 *As with a breaking of my bones, My enemies reproach me, While they say to me all day long, "Where is your God?"* 11 *Why are you cast down, O my soul? And why are you disquieted within me? Hope in God; For I shall yet praise Him, The help of my countenance and my God. Psalm 42:9-11*

They end, by identifying God as their Rock. They don't ignore their inner turmoil; they still confess that they:
1. Feel forgotten by God.
2. Are mourning because of the oppression of their enemies.

Notice that although their situation and their emotional condition has not yet changed, they continue to push pass their feelings and encourage themselves in the Lord.

Encourage yourself in the Beauty of who God is, not in what He can do for you.

Lesson 4:
"Equipped to Fight the Spirit of Heaviness"

Review

In the previous lesson, depression was compared to an unquenchable thirst that only God can satisfy. Psalm 42 guided us in finding relief from unhappiness. We learned to:

☐ Depend on God's affirmation and not man's.

☐ Remember all God has done for us personally.

☐ Encourage ourselves to Hope in God.

☐ Praise God continually, knowing we can expect to experience Him, even in the midst of pain.

Objectives:

1. To recognize depression as a spirit of heaviness.
2. To be equipped with spiritual weapons.

In Lesson 2 we discussed Jesus' ability to heal our emotional wounds and any chemical imbalance in our brain.

> *He (Jesus) is equally in the business of healing our emotional wounds and any physical ailment (this includes our outer body, every organ, cell and chemical inside our body). Lesson 2 p.20*

Now, we will focus on walking in victory over the spiritual side of depression. Isaiah 61:3, says He gives us,

"...the garment of praise for the spirit of heaviness..."

Remember:

> *The word derived from Latin that we get the word depressed from means to PRESS DOWN. It is difficult to fight this battle on your own, because it literally feels like a physical, emotional and spiritual weight pressing you down, causing you to think that you are unable to lift your hands and move forward.*
> *Lesson 1 p.8*

Group Activity (15 minutes)
Discuss the following two questions and write your personal answer.

Did you know that depression or prolonged sadness is a spirit of heaviness?

_____

Draw a picture of the first thing that comes to your mind, when you hear, spirit of heaviness.

Do physical solutions (i.e. exercise, eating right, medication) solve spiritual problems?

_____

_____

Imagine yourself standing on a battlefield, only having use of two of your five senses, hearing and feeling (touch). Certainly you don't need to smell or taste, to have victory, but how can you fight and win a battle without sight? **On the spiritual battlefield, you are unable to see your enemy because he is invisible.**

You can <u>hear</u>:
➢ Your thoughts of sadness and grief.
➢ The voice of your enemy telling you, "Give up, there's no hope, just quit living, quit trying! You're worthless, useless, you've already lost!"

You can <u>feel</u>:
➢ Depression "your enemy" as a pressing weight in your mind, heart and body.
➢ Loss of energy and determination.
➢ Your faith slowly slipping.

In 2 Corinthians 10:3-5, Apostle Paul teaches how to use invisible weapons on our unseen opponent.

> *For though we walk in the flesh, we do not war after the flesh: 2 Corinthians 10:3*

Since, you are fighting with an invisible being, you can't use your fist to punch him, or feet to kick him, a gun to shoot him, or a knife to cut him.

URGENT WARNING: *You must realize that you are not your enemy. He will try to influence you to hurt yourself through cutting, overdosing, hanging, shooting yourself, etc.; All this will be done, in your physical effort to stop your emotional pain. Should you experience these thoughts, call the National Suicide Prevention Lifeline at 1-800-273-8255, immediately.*

In a spiritual battle, it is important to understand that **since GOD exists, the spirit realm, comprising of angels and demons, also exists; these demons will try to oppress you, thankfully you're victory comes in believing in Christ and the authority that you have because He lives in you.** *(If you have not accepted Christ as your savior, now would be the perfect time to invite Him to be Lord of your life)*

For the weapons of our warfare are not carnal, but mighty through God to the pulling down of strong holds; 2 Corinthians 10:4

A stronghold is a high place, a refuge, where you are protected from attack. In this scenario, the enemy establishes strongholds in your mind, to protect himself in your life. The adversary disguises himself as an angel of light (he likes to wear masks) so that he is unnoticed and welcomed. He whispers lies that cause us to doubt ourselves, as well as, God's existence, faithfulness and love. As you uncover these lies, victory comes when you stop believing them. Through Christ you have the power to pull down every demonic stronghold.

Group Activity (15 minutes)
List a few lies you have believed about yourself and God. Share your list, as you feel comfortable.

_____

_____

_____

_____

> **Casting down imaginations, and every high thing that exalteth itself against the knowledge of God, and bringing into captivity every thought to the obedience of Christ; 2 Corinthians 10:5**

Anything you believe that is the opposite of what the Bible says about you, *needs to be removed from the throne of your mind and heart;* through faith filled prayers, meditation on God's Word and declarations.

"Death and life are in the power of the tongue: and they that love it shall eat the fruit thereof."
Proverbs 18:21

To win, you must differentiate between whether what you hear, think, believe and say, elevates God or comes against His Word. *Victory comes as you choose to believe and declare God's truth over your life.* Make time to read the Bible, so you can learn what God says about Himself, about you and about your adversary, the devil.

Often times, it is challenging to bring ALL OF OUR THOUGHTS into obedience to Christ. The reality is, our thoughts will take us to the darkest, dirtiest places of our heart as well as to the brightest hopes and dreams we have for ourselves and others.

Will you accept God's challenge and help to submit the thoughts that are damaging you, to Christ?

_____

_____

_____

_____

STOP IMAGINING YOURSELF AS DEFEATED.

See Jesus stepping on the battlefield with you and have confidence that He has given you the VICTORY!

He conquered all realms of power at His death and resurrection. The same faith that leads you to salvation is the same faith that leads you to a victorious life.

> *"Which he wrought in Christ, when he raised him from the dead, and set him at his own right hand in the heavenly places, 21 Far above all principality, and power, and might, and dominion, and every name that is named, not only in this world, but also in that which is to come: 22 And hath put all things under his feet, and gave him to be the head over all things to the church,"*
> *Ephesians 1:20-22*

Now, close your eyes, and extend your hands towards heaven, by faith, whisper a personal prayer and receive the victory that Christ conquered for you and put inside of your heart.

Heavenly Father, thank you for giving me everything I need to be victorious in Christ. Forgive me for every time I have chosen to believe the lies of the enemy, instead of your truth. Please give me a hunger to learn your Word and an increased faith to believe and apply it in my life, in Jesus name.

Lesson 5:
"The Great Exchange"

Review
In the previous lesson, depression was identified as the *spirit of heaviness*. You gained victory in your spiritual battles with it, by:
- ☐ Understanding you are not your enemy.
- ☐ Uncovering and ceasing to believe the devil's lies.
- ☐ Replacing damaging thoughts with God's truth.

Objective:
1. Understand God's care for those who mourn.
2. Exchange your pain for Christ's pleasures.

In Luke 4:16-19 Jesus stood in a synagogue and read Isaiah 61:1-3.
*"The Spirit of the Lord GOD is upon me; because the LORD hath anointed me to preach good tidings unto the meek; he hath sent me to **bind up the brokenhearted, to proclaim liberty to the captives, and the opening of the prison to them that are bound***; 2 *To proclaim the acceptable year of the LORD, and the day of vengeance of our God;* **to comfort all that mourn;** 3 **To appoint unto them that mourn in Zion, to give unto them beauty for ashes, the oil of joy for mourning, the garment of praise for the spirit of heaviness**; *that they might be called trees of righteousness, the planting of the LORD, that he might be glorified."*

God demonstrates the magnitude of His care!
- ➤ He is our comforter.
- ➤ He exchanges our pain with pleasure.
- ➤ He frees and heals us from every emotional prison.
- ➤ He plants us in fertile soil for His glory.
- ➤ He preaches a message of good news.

Did you know that Christ promised not to leave us comfortless? In John 14:16-18, He speaks of Holy Spirit, our comforter, living with us and in us.

*"And I will pray the Father, and he shall give you another Comforter, that he may abide with you for ever; Even the Spirit of truth; whom the world cannot receive, because it seeth him not, neither knoweth him: but ye know him; for he dwelleth with you, and shall be in you. **I will not leave you comfortless: I will come to you**."*

In Isaiah 61:2-3, a specific group of people are identified. These are those who mourn. In Matthew 5:4, Jesus said, *"Blessed are they that mourn: for they shall be comforted."* All of us, at some point, will face the indescribable grief one experiences when a love one dies.

In Genesis 37:34-35, at the false news of his son's, Joseph, death, Jacob responded this way, *"Then Jacob tore his clothes, put on sackcloth and **mourned for his son many days**. All his sons and daughters came to comfort him, but **he refused to be comforted.** "No," he said, "I will continue to mourn **until I join my son in the grave**." So his father wept for him."*

Years later, at the thought of the possibility of losing another son, Jacob said, *"... My son shall not go down with you; for his brother is dead, and he is left alone: if mischief befall him by the way in which ye go, then shall ye bring down my gray hairs with **sorrow to the grave**."(Genesis 42:38)*

For some, the grief of death, when prolonged, may cause them to spiral into a deep depression. The longing to be where that person is, may create a desire to join him/her in death. In Lesson 1 we learned the importance of having a Support System. If you are grieving the loss of a loved one, consider visiting **www.GriefShare.org** for encouragement and to attend an ongoing support group.

In Thessalonians 4:13-18 we are encouraged and comforted in knowing that we will be reunited with our loved ones who die in Christ. Although, this truth does not take the *initial pain of grief away*, it serves as comfort and a guardrail. Paul tells us that we do not have to grieve as though we have no hope.

HOPE IS THE GUARDRAIL THAT HELPS US MOVE FORWARD IN PURPOSE AND NOT ABORT OUR MISSION IN LIFE.

At times we are tempted to crawl over the guardrail. But, don't do it! In your present pain, resist the urge to make an impulsive decision that can affect your future. Don't allow sorrow to prophecy a future of death or stagnation, to you. Push forward in HOPE.

"But I would not have you to be ignorant, brethren, concerning them which are asleep, that ye sorrow not, even as others which have no hope. 14 For if we believe that Jesus died and rose again, even so them also which sleep in Jesus will God bring with him. 15 For this we say unto you by the word of the Lord, that we which are alive and remain unto the coming of the Lord shall not prevent them which are asleep. 16 For the Lord himself shall descend from heaven with a shout, with the voice of the archangel, and with the trump of God: and the dead in Christ shall rise first: 17 Then we which are alive and remain shall be

caught up together with them in the clouds, to meet the Lord in the air: and so shall we ever be with the Lord. 18 Wherefore comfort one another with these words."

For others, though no one has died, he/she lives with this same intense feeling of loss, perhaps as a result of a traumatic life event, a divorce, the end of a friendship, physical illness; loss of limbs, job, home or finances and more.

Proverbs 13:12 states, *"Hope deferred maketh the heart sick: but when the desire cometh, it is a tree of life."* Since our emotions are directly impacted when there is a delay in receiving what we are hoping for; it can be a challenge, as we wait on God to change our situations. When God in His perfect timing steps in and satisfies us, Solomon says it is a *tree of life.* In Nehemiah 8:10 we learn that the joy of the Lord is our strength. An influx of joy floods our souls when our hope comes alive.

Grief drains you, but

JOY STRENGTHENS YOU.

Grief tempts you to die prematurely, but

JOY FILLS YOU WITH HOPE FOR THE FUTURE.

Group Activity (15 minutes)
Answer the questions, then discuss with the group.

Have you mourned the loss of a loved one or friend?
If yes, how long has the grieving process been?

_____

_____

_____

_____

_____

_____

_____

Has anything occurred in your life, unrelated to
death, which brought about the feeling of
mourning? If yes, what transpired?

_____

_____

_____

_____

_____

_____

_____

Ash is the powdery remainder of something that has been burned. How many moments in your life have been burned?

Take this moment to imagine *your ashes* as every fragment of disappointment, hurt, loneliness, and loss, feeling misunderstood, pain, rejection, sadness and shame. List some of your burnt areas.

_____

_____

_____

_____

This dark ash takes up residence in our minds and shades our thoughts. It taints the way we see and value ourselves. Christ came to give us *beauty for our ashes*. He has promised to replace our ashes with something attractive. The Hebrew word used for beauty in this verse is *pe'er*, according to Strong's Definitions, it is *an embellishment, i.e. fancy head-dress:-beauty, bonnet, godly, ornament, tire*. Jesus is in the trading industry.

Jesus will exchange His *Crown of Beauty* for your *Crown of Ashes*.

Will you receive this gift from the Lord?

_____

Let's pray.

Heavenly Father, I give you the ashes of my pain and choose to receive the beautiful crown you have for me. I believe that it represents your Lordship over my life, the helmet of salvation. As I study Your Word, help me to develop the mind of Christ, in Jesus name.

THE GREAT ECXHANGE

In Lesson 4 we highlighted the *spirit of heaviness*. It's time to look at its' replacement, the Garment of Praise. The Lord wants to change your wardrobe by **removing the heavy, dark coat of depression and replacing it with a light weight, free flowing garment**. This new apparel brings liberty.

Praise is Powerful, it:
- Causes our minds to magnify Christ above everything and everyone.
- Shows God that we honor Him for who He is and all He does.
- Is an invitation to God to move on our behalves.

In Acts 16, Paul and Silas were wrongfully beaten and chained in a dark prison. Their condition, would have justified their need to cry, complain and meditate on their sufferings. And maybe they did, for a little while, but not too long after, they exchanged their bloodied garments for the Garment of Praise. It is recorded, *"And at midnight Paul and Silas prayed, and sang praises unto God: and the prisoners heard them. And suddenly there was a great earthquake, so that the foundations of the prison were shaken: and immediately all the doors were opened, and every one's bands were loosed." (Acts 16:25-26)*

The result of their praise not only loosed their own chains, but the chains of those around them.

Are you ready for a wardrobe change?

As you start each day, tell the Lord, thank you and ask Him to clothe you in His Garment of Praise.

"Enter into his gates with thanksgiving, and into his courts with praise: be thankful unto him, and bless his name." Psalm 100:4

OIL OF JOY

Our mourning moves the heart of God, so deeply, that He made a remedy called the Oil of Joy. In the Bible, great significance is given to oil, such as anointing (separating) someone to serve God in the role of King, Priest or Prophet; healing wounds, as well as praying for the healing of others. James 5:14 instructs, *"Is any sick among you? Let him call for the elders of the church; and let them pray over him, **anointing him with oil** in the name of the Lord:"*

JOY...
- Comes from Abiding in Jesus.
- Is found in salvation, the hope of eternal life and the presence of God. In John 15:11, Jesus said, *"These things have I spoken unto you, that my joy might remain in you, and that your joy may be full."*
- Results from having the fruit of Holy Spirit.
- Deepens as our relationship with Christ deepens.

The psalmists sang to the Lord,

"Thou wilt shew me the path of life: in thy presence is fullness of joy; at thy right hand there are pleasures for evermore." Psalm 16:11

"And my soul shall be joyful in the LORD: it shall rejoice in his salvation". - Psalm 35:9

Restore unto me the joy of thy salvation; and uphold me with thy free spirit. Psalm 51:12

Experiencing God's joy does not guarantee that we won't have difficult days and tearful moments. Why?

Because the battlefield is not only for fighting.

It is also for training.

During our battles,

WE MATURE IN CHARACTER AND PERSPECTIVE.

Let's pray.

Heavenly Father, pour on me Your Oil of Joy, may it be my strength, when mourning tries to drain me, in Jesus name.

Lesson 6:
"Empowered to Renew Your Mind"

Review
In the previous lesson, we learned that,
- ☐ Christ cares deeply for those in mourning and has given us Holy Spirit to comfort us.
- ☐ We must resist the urge to make impulsive decisions in our present pain.
- ☐ Christ has provided a great exchange for us. Beauty for ashes, a garment of praise for a spirit of heaviness, and the oil of joy, for mourning.

Objective:
1. Accept God as our stronghold.
2. Learn healthy ways to cope with sadness.
3. Learn to comfort others.

God is Our Stronghold

In Lesson 4, we discussed the strongholds that the enemy establishes, when we believe his lies. They are like castles in our minds, where he guards himself through fear, sadness, unbelief, etc. We know that combining the mighty weapons God has equipped us with and prayer, we can bulldoze every ungodly structure that has been fortified in our minds.

A stronghold is a high place, a refuge, where you are protected from attack. In this scenario, the enemy establishes strongholds in your mind, to protect himself in your life. The adversary disguises himself as an angel of light (he likes to wear masks) so that he is unnoticed and welcomed. He whispers lies that cause us to doubt ourselves, as well as, God's existence, faithfulness and love. As you uncover these lies, victory comes when you stop believing them. Through Christ you have the power to pull down every demonic stronghold. Lesson 4 pg. 32

There is a stronghold, however, that we need, and his name is Jesus! King David explains in Psalm 18:2 (NKJV).

"The LORD *is my rock and my fortress and my deliverer; My God, my strength, in whom I will trust; my shield and the horn of my salvation,*
MY STRONGHOLD.

God invites us to trust Him as our safe place, where His presence makes up the walls of the castle in our hearts and minds. In this stronghold we are not imprisoned, but free to abide in the security of His unconditional love. Here, we are protected and empowered to face our brokenness through Him *and have a renewed mind every day.*

In each lesson our minds are being renewed through the Word of God and the power of His Holy Spirit. We learn from Romans 12:2 that the Lord wants to transform the way we think.

"And be not conformed to this world: but be ye transformed by the renewing of your mind, that ye may prove what is that good, and acceptable, and perfect, will of God."

Have you noticed that your brain has a default mode that your feelings revert to?

_____

_____

Although it is a constant battle to control our thoughts, we must make the commitment and choose daily, to shift to the renewed mode of our brain.

48

Group Activity (15 minutes)

List some old ways of thinking you have had, then replace it, with renewed thoughts. Share your list, as you feel comfortable.

OLD THOUGHTS	RENEWED THOUGHTS

Unhealthy/Healthy Ways of Coping with Sadness

Let's identify some **Unhealthy Ways** we may be dealing with sadness, grief and depression:

- ☐ Staying silent about it.
- ☐ Pretending everything is ok.
- ☐ Ignoring your personal pain.
- ☐ Attempting to relieve pain by physically harming yourself (self-mutilation).
- ☐ Attempting to relieve pain by coming up with a plan to end your life.
- ☐ Using people and substances to make you feel happy and to numb your pain.
- ☐ Feeding your pain by listening to sad music and watching sad shows.
- ☐ Isolating yourself.
- ☐ _____

If you identified with any of the options above, it's time to stand in front of a "trash can" and throw every unhealthy coping mechanism away. But wait, it's not enough to just throw them away, you must replace those spaces in your life that those thoughts and behaviors have taken up with **Healthy Ways** to deal with sadness, grief and depression:

- ☐ Pray.
- ☐ Talk to the "right" someone about it.
- ☐ Take off your mask, be honest with yourself.
- ☐ Examine your pain, identify its source, journal about it and share with someone you trust.
- ☐ Exercise and Eat tryptophan filled foods.
- ☐ Read the Holy Bible.
- ☐ Listen to uplifting music/watch uplifting shows.
- ☐ Spend time with others.
- ☐ _____

Don't Be Afraid to Comfort Others

There is a special strength that comes over us, when we use the tools we have been equipped with, to benefit others. As we heal, one day at a time, our experiences/testimonies will assist others to walk through their valley seasons victoriously.

Your present pain does not disqualify you from impacting and empowering someone else.

As we are comforted by the Lord, we are able to bring comfort to others. In 2 Corinthians 1:3-4, Apostle Paul encourages us, *"Blessed be the God, even Father of our Lord Jesus Christ, the Father of mercies and the God of all comfort; 4 who comforteth us in all our tribulation, that we may be able to comfort them which are in any trouble, by the comfort wherewith we ourselves are comforted of God."*

You may just be the Support System someone else needs. Often times, knowing that our presence brings hope to another, encourages us to live another day.

Should you need someone to talk with, when you are struggling between your default mode and renewed mode, consider scheduling a Biblical teletherapy appointment at www.houseofprotection.org.

Let's take a moment to pray.
Heavenly Father, I need you to be my stronghold. When my mind tries to revert to its default mode, give me the discipline to shift back into a renewed mode and to choose to handle my emotions in healthy ways. Please give me the courage to share my story with others, so that I may bring comfort to them, in their times of grief, in Jesus name.

As we come to the end of our lessons in Defeating Depression, let's remember all we have learned.

- ☐ **Identify Depression.**
- ☐ **Remove Your Mask(s).**
- ☐ **Seek out a Support System.**
- ☐ **Pray.**
- ☐ **Confront Depression.**
- ☐ **Adjust Your Perspective.**
- ☐ **Believe Jesus can heal your heart and brain.**
- ☐ **Depend on the Affirmation of God.**
- ☐ **Remember and Reflect on all God has done.**
- ☐ **Recognize Depression as a spirit of heaviness.**
- ☐ **Understand you are not your enemy.**
- ☐ **Cease to believe the devil's lies.**
- ☐ **Replace damaging thoughts with God's truth.**
- ☐ **Know God cares for those who mourn.**
- ☐ **Exchange your pain for Christ's comfort, beauty, garment of praise and His oil of joy.**
- ☐ **Trust God as Your Stronghold.**
- ☐ **Choose Healthy ways to cope with sadness.**
- ☐ **Comfort Others.**

Go through this guide as often as you need to and hold on to the promises of God.

*He that dwelleth in the secret place of the Most High shall abide under the shadow of the Almighty.
I will say of the LORD, "He is my refuge and my fortress; my God; in Him I will trust." Psalm 91:1-2*

The LORD is nigh unto them that are of a broken heart; and saveth such as be of a contrite spirit. Psalm 34:18

And the peace of God, which passeth all understanding, shall keep your hearts and minds through Christ Jesus. Philippians 4:7

Visit **WWW.HOUSEOFPROTECTION.ORG** to avail yourself of other courses in the **Overcoming Life's Obstacles Series**.

A Biblical Guide to
Anger & Conflict Resolution

A Biblical Guide to
Confronting & Conquering Fear & Anxiety

A Biblical Guide to
Defeating Depression

A Biblical Guide to
Healing from Rejection and Abandonment

A Biblical Guide to
Knowing Your Identity & Purpose

Go to **WWW.SUZANNEMARCELLUS.COM** to find books in the Developing the Fruit of the Spirit, A Journey Through the Heart of Christ series, written by Suzanne Phillippa Marcellus.

Developing the Fruit of the Spirit, A Journey Through the Heart of Christ

(Available in print and audio)

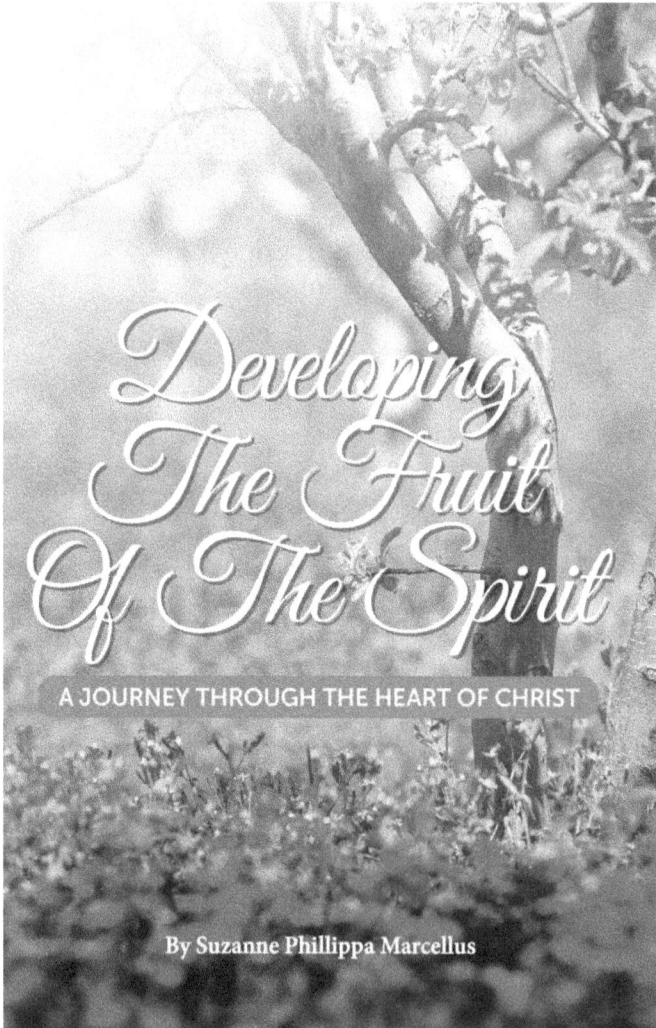

Developing the Fruit of Love
30 Day Devotional

Developing the Fruit of Joy
30 Day Devotional

Developing the Fruit of Peace
30 Day Devotional

Developing the Fruit of Patience Longsuffering
30 Day Devotional

Developing the Fruit of Kindness
30 Day Devotional

Developing the Fruit of Goodness
30 Day Devotional

Developing the Fruit of Faithfulness Faith
30 Day Devotional

Developing the Fruit of Gentleness Meekness
30 Day Devotional

Developing the Fruit of Self-Control
30 Day Devotional

Developing the Fruit of Righteousness
30 Day Devotional

Developing the Fruit of Justice
30 Day Devotional

Developing the Fruit of Mercy
30 Day Devotional

MORE ABOUT THE AUTHOR

Suzanne was given a vision by the Lord in 2002 to counsel, disciple, educate and house hurting children and teens. House of Protection, Inc., is a Christian, 501(C) 3 organization, in operation since May 2004.

WWW.HOUSEOFPROTECTION.ORG

We are a refuge of hope for children, teens and families, providing Counseling, Life Empowerment Resources and a future Residential Program for youth ages 5-18.

MISSION STATEMENT
To be a safe place where children and families are equipped and empowered to overcome life obstacles, as we guide them to their God given purpose.

VISION
To have global impact by providing Counseling, Life Empowerment Resources and homes where children are nurtured and educated.